Aa Bb Cc Dd Ee
Ff Gg Hh Ii Jj Kk
Ll Mm Nn Oo Pp
Qq Rr Ss Tt Uu
Vv Ww Xx Yy Zz

The A to Z of Mistakes
Every Opps Can Help Me Grow

Written and illustrated by Tenille Dowe

Copyright © 2025 Tenille Dowe

All rights reserved. No part of this book may be reproduced in any manner whatsoever without prior written permission of the publisher.

First Printing, 2025

Published by Creative Heart Connection
www.creativeheartconnection.com

ISBN 978-1-7641624-4-9

The A to Z of Mistakes

Every Oops Can Help Me Grow

Written and Illustrated by Tenille Dowe

Mistakes are part of learning

Everyone makes mistakes. Big ones, small ones, funny ones, messy ones.

This book is your A–Z guide to why mistakes aren't the end, they're the beginning of learning.

Aa

A is for - Acting too fast......

I bounded in the way roos do, an impulsive, angry rush, with no clue.

When I pause before I leap, smart thinking keeps me out of trouble deep.

Bb

B is for - Brown Bear Breaking something..........

I dropped a teacup, its shattered pieces spread.
Glued with gleaming golden seams, it shone with strength instead.
So broken things don't trouble me, they mend and grow with dignity.

Cc

C is for – Cockatoo colouring outside the lines……….

My colours danced beyond the frame, soft blooms that changed like living flame.

I learned that creativity grows the moment I let all the borders go.

Dd

D is for – Dog dropping a ball....

I missed the catch and heard it fall.
A silly pup who lost the ball.
Mistakes ring loud but help build my skills.

They sharpen my focus with patience and will.

Ee

E is for – Elephant eating too much……

I ate the peanuts, every bite
and felt a mighty ache that night.
My belly whispered,
for goodness' sake……
You need to learn just when to take a break.

F is for – Frog forgetting....

I'm just a frog who hopped away and left my homework due Friday.
Five flies to catch... but forgot!
With planning now, and notes I jot.........

I find it helps me quite a lot.

G g

G is for – Goat guessing wrong.......

I chose a path a goat might take.......and picked the wrong one by mistake.

But sometimes wrong leads into right, each stumble sharpens inner sight.

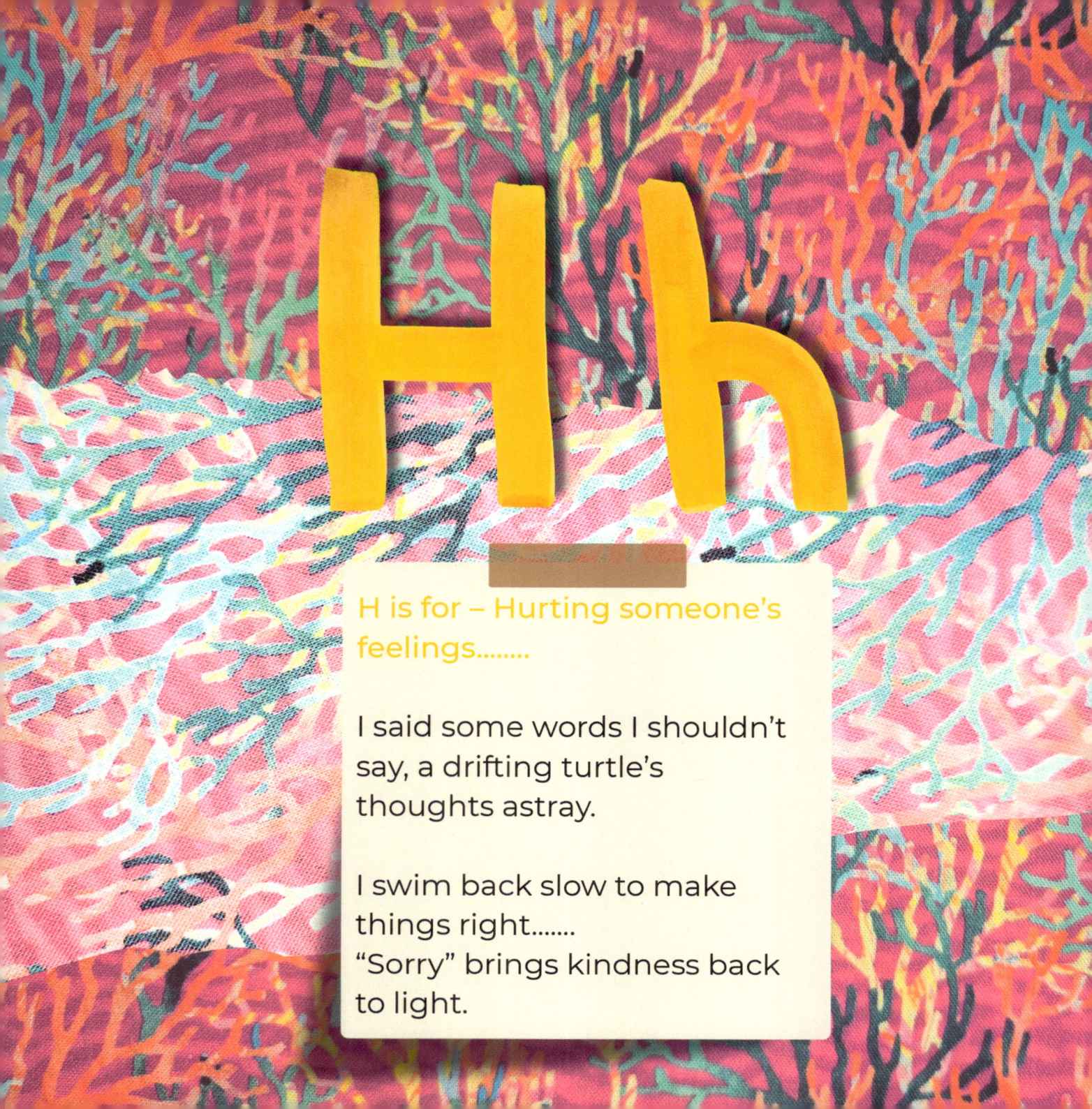

H is for – Hurting someone's feelings........

I said some words I shouldn't say, a drifting turtle's thoughts astray.

I swim back slow to make things right.......
"Sorry" brings kindness back to light.

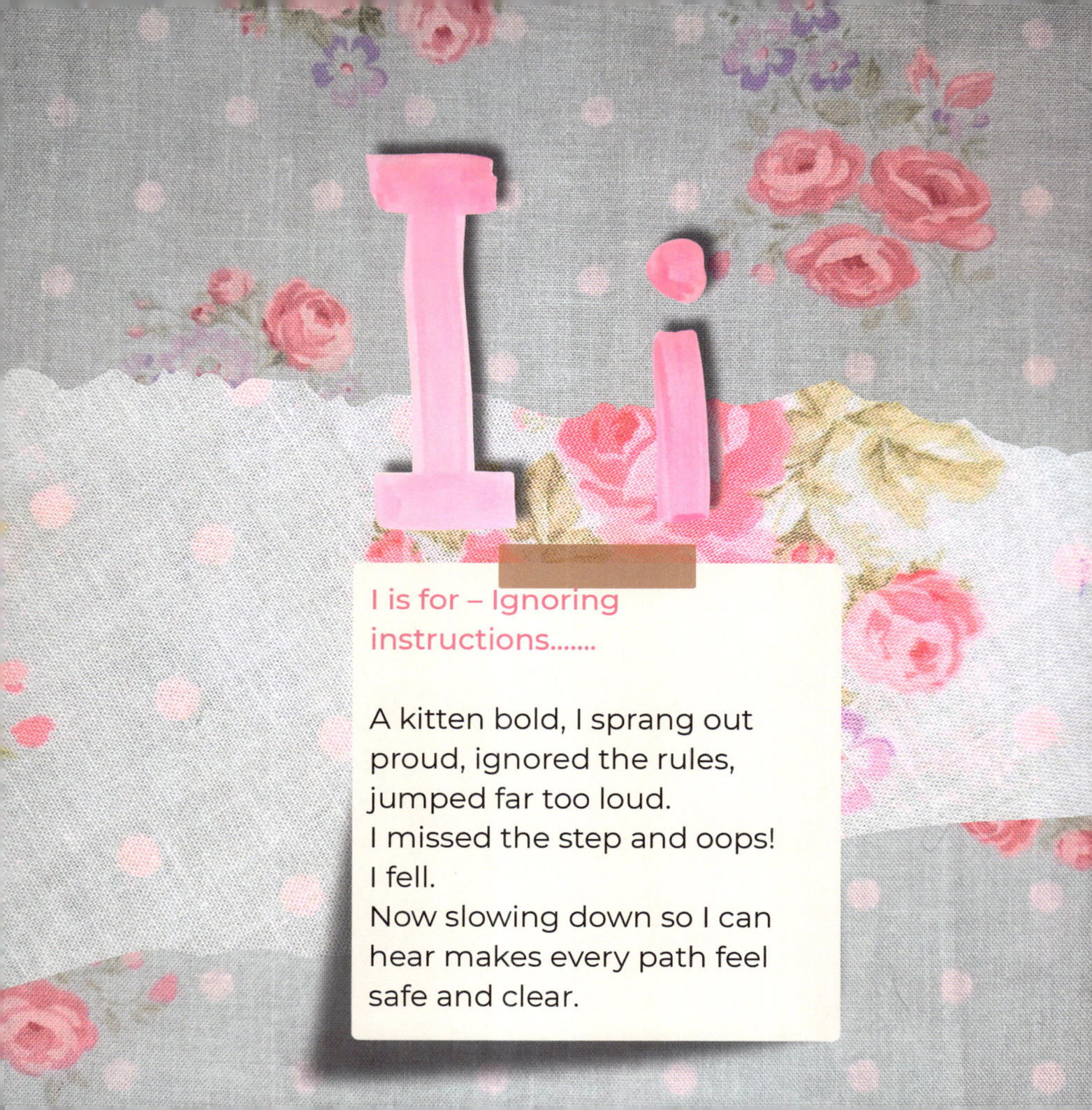

Ii

I is for – Ignoring instructions…….

A kitten bold, I sprang out proud, ignored the rules, jumped far too loud.
I missed the step and oops! I fell.
Now slowing down so I can hear makes every path feel safe and clear.

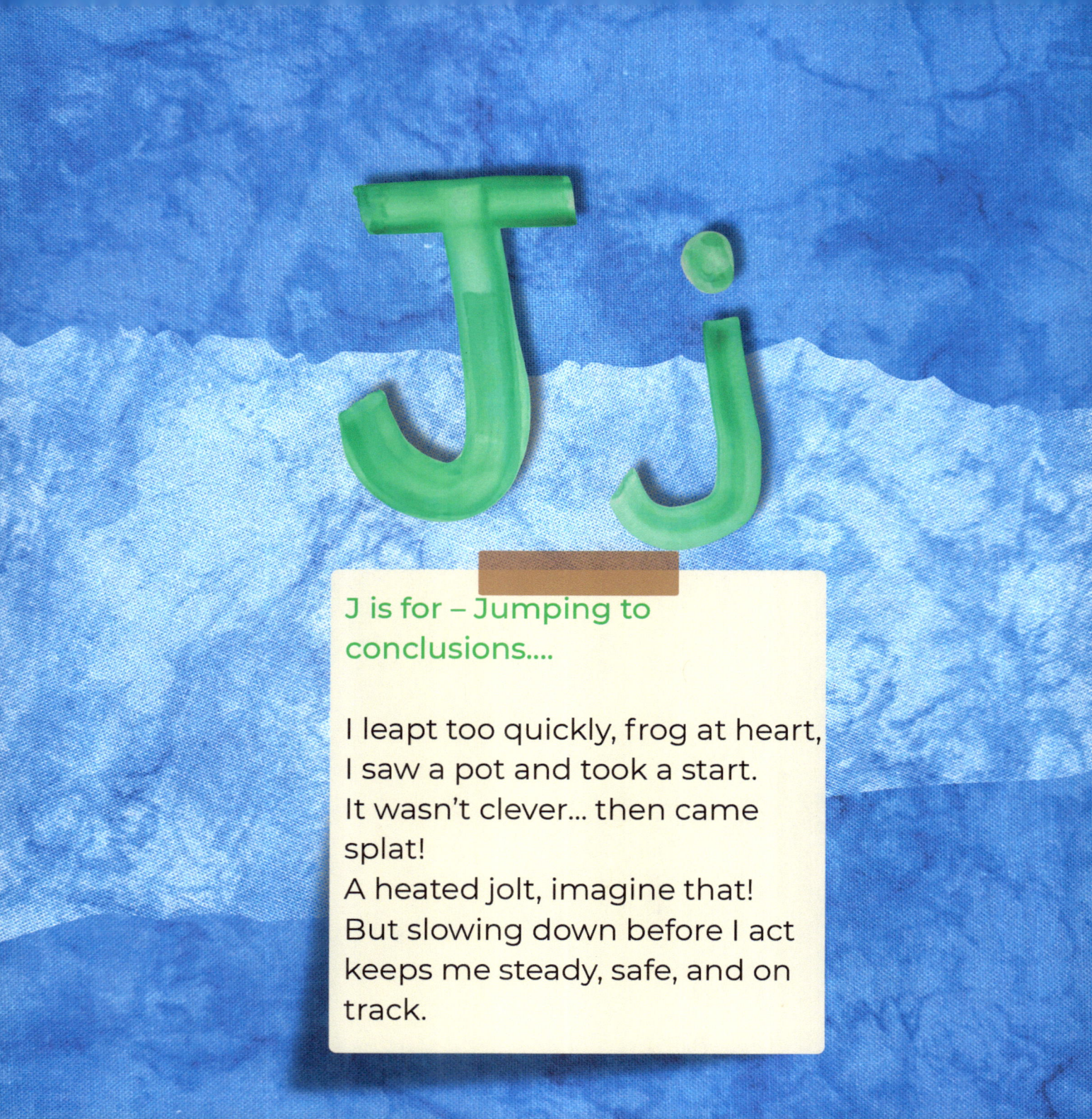

J is for – Jumping to conclusions....

I leapt too quickly, frog at heart,
I saw a pot and took a start.
It wasn't clever... then came splat!
A heated jolt, imagine that!
But slowing down before I act keeps me steady, safe, and on track.

K is for – Keeping quiet when I need help.......

I'm a blue yabby caught on a hook, too shy to ask for help and too scared to look.

I wriggle, I'm stuck,
until I see, that asking for help could set me free.

Ll

L is for – Losing something………

An old toy dog,
that's simply me.
I lost my own eye,
one, two… then three.

Yet losing things has helped me
find, the care we owe to ours
and yours and mine.

M is for – Making a big mess………

I'm just a pink pig splashing through.
A muddy mess from snout to my shoe.

Sometimes, mess is how I find the brightest ideas and creativity in my mind.

N is for – Not knowing how to start….

I am a turtle with a great big heart, unsure of how to even make a start.

Taking one small step with support that day, helped me begin and find my own way.

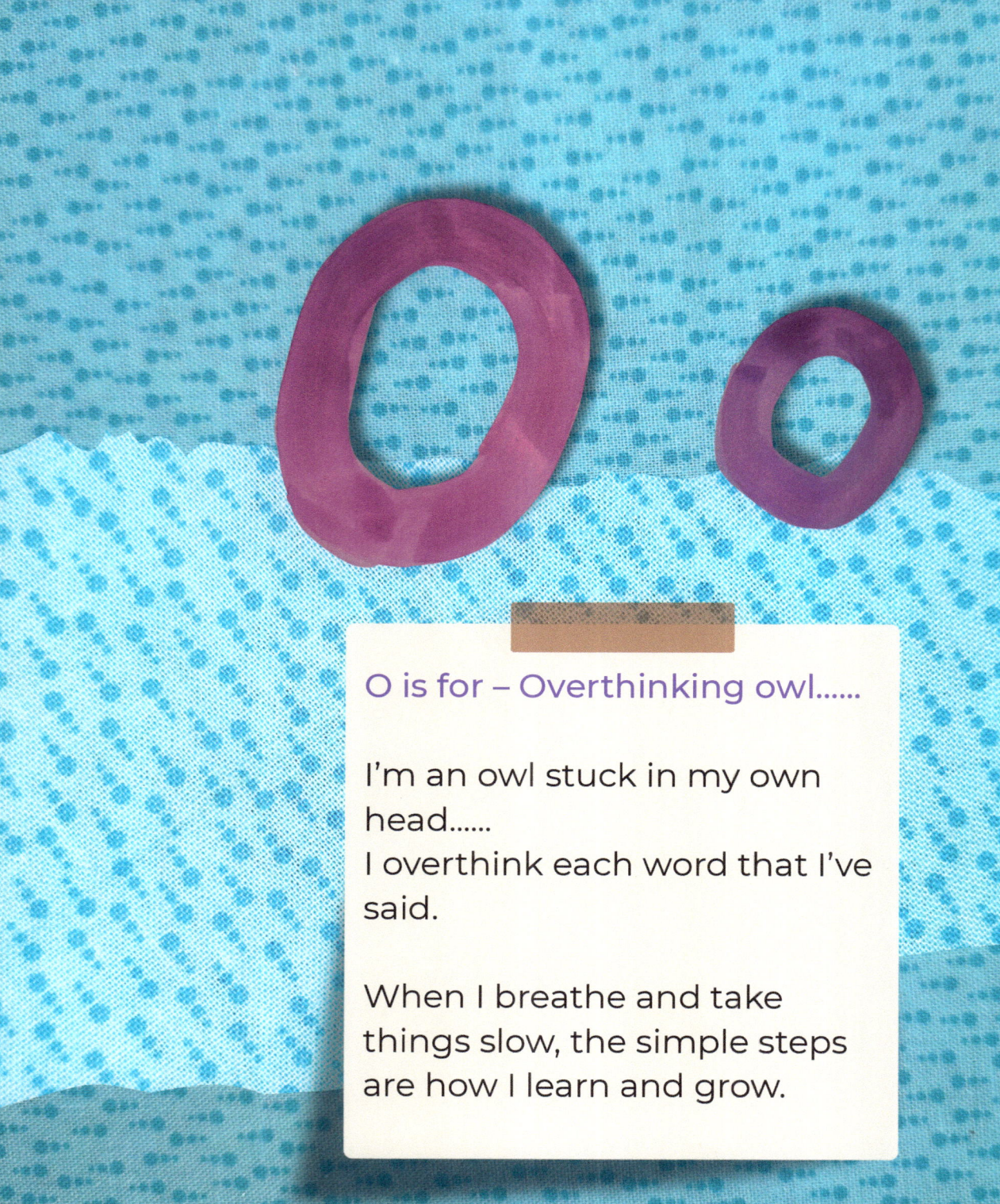

O is for – Overthinking owl……

I'm an owl stuck in my own head……
I overthink each word that I've said.

When I breathe and take things slow, the simple steps are how I learn and grow.

Pp

P – Picking the wrong choice.......

I'm a goldfish who turned the wrong way.
I swam left, when I should've gone right that day.
Every mix-up helps me see, the smart choices that make sense for me.

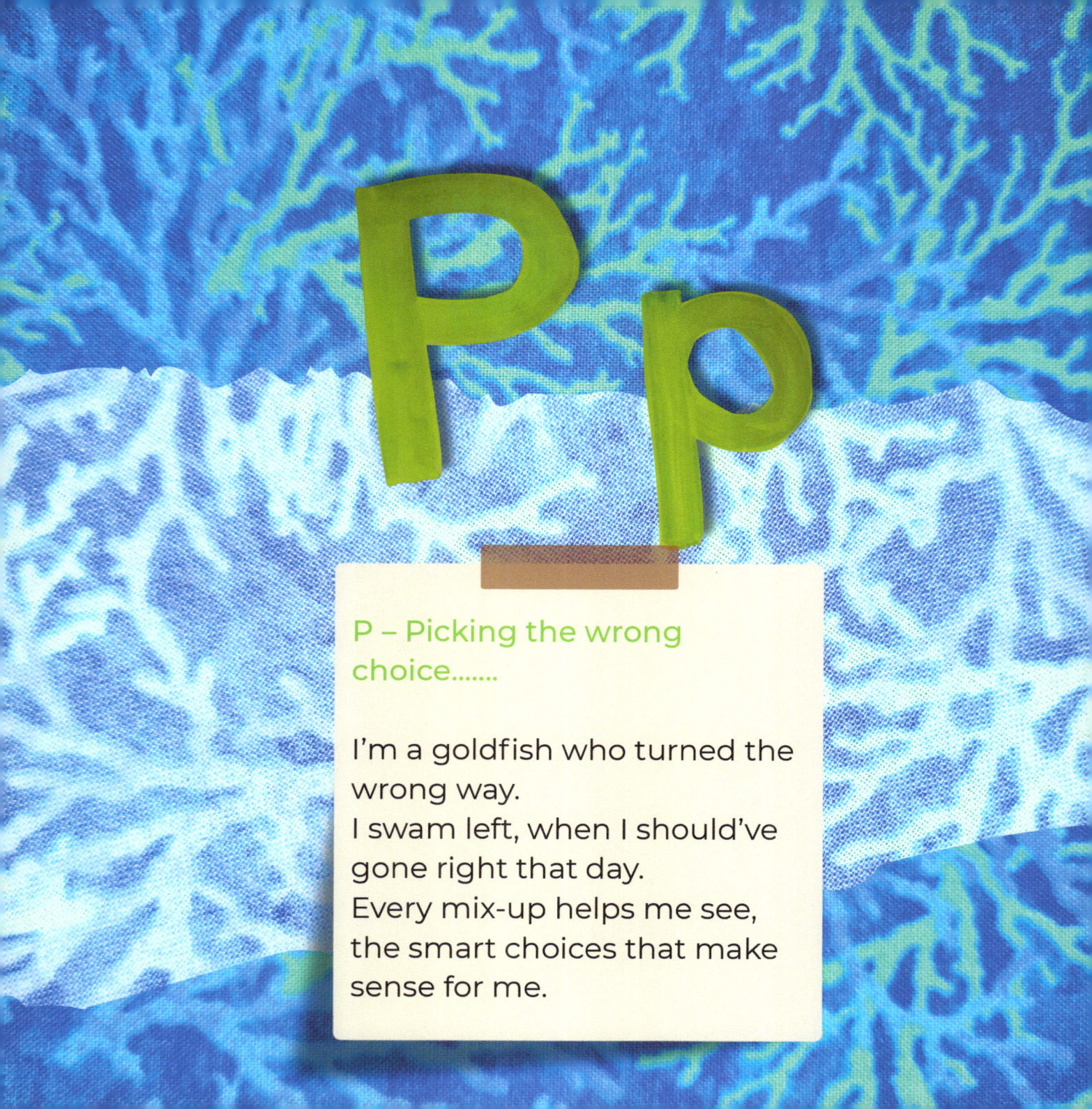

Q is for – Quitting too soon……

I'm an old teddy with a half-done heart, I stitched a bit, then chose to part.

When I try and see things through, my heart feels whole in everything I do.

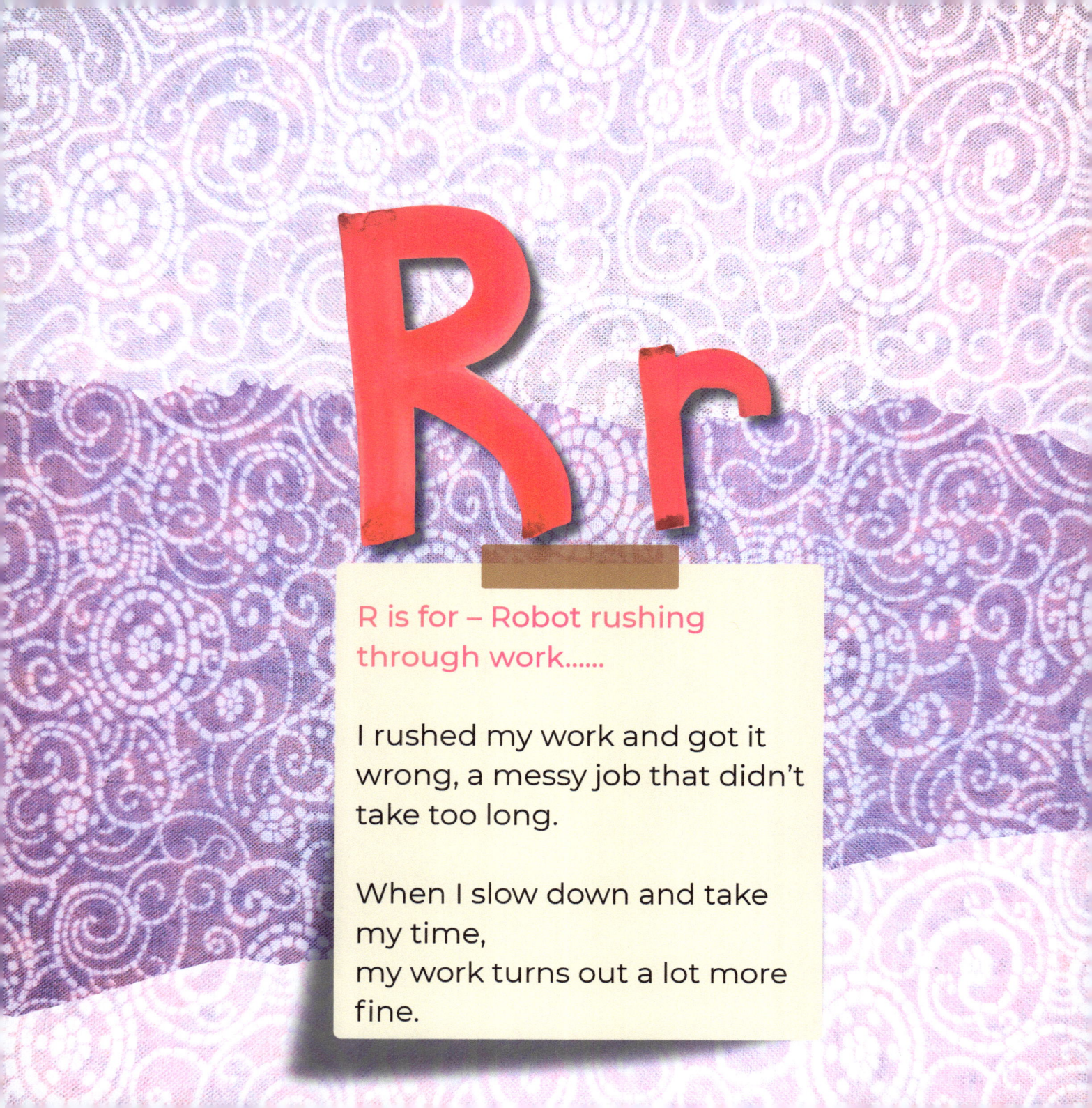

R is for – Robot rushing through work……

I rushed my work and got it wrong, a messy job that didn't take too long.

When I slow down and take my time,
my work turns out a lot more fine.

Ss

S is for – Spilling watercolour everywhere......

I'm a seal with bright, splash-happy paint.
One swoosh sends colours like a wild complaint!
Every spill teaches me to move with care.
Next time I'll paint with calmness in the air.

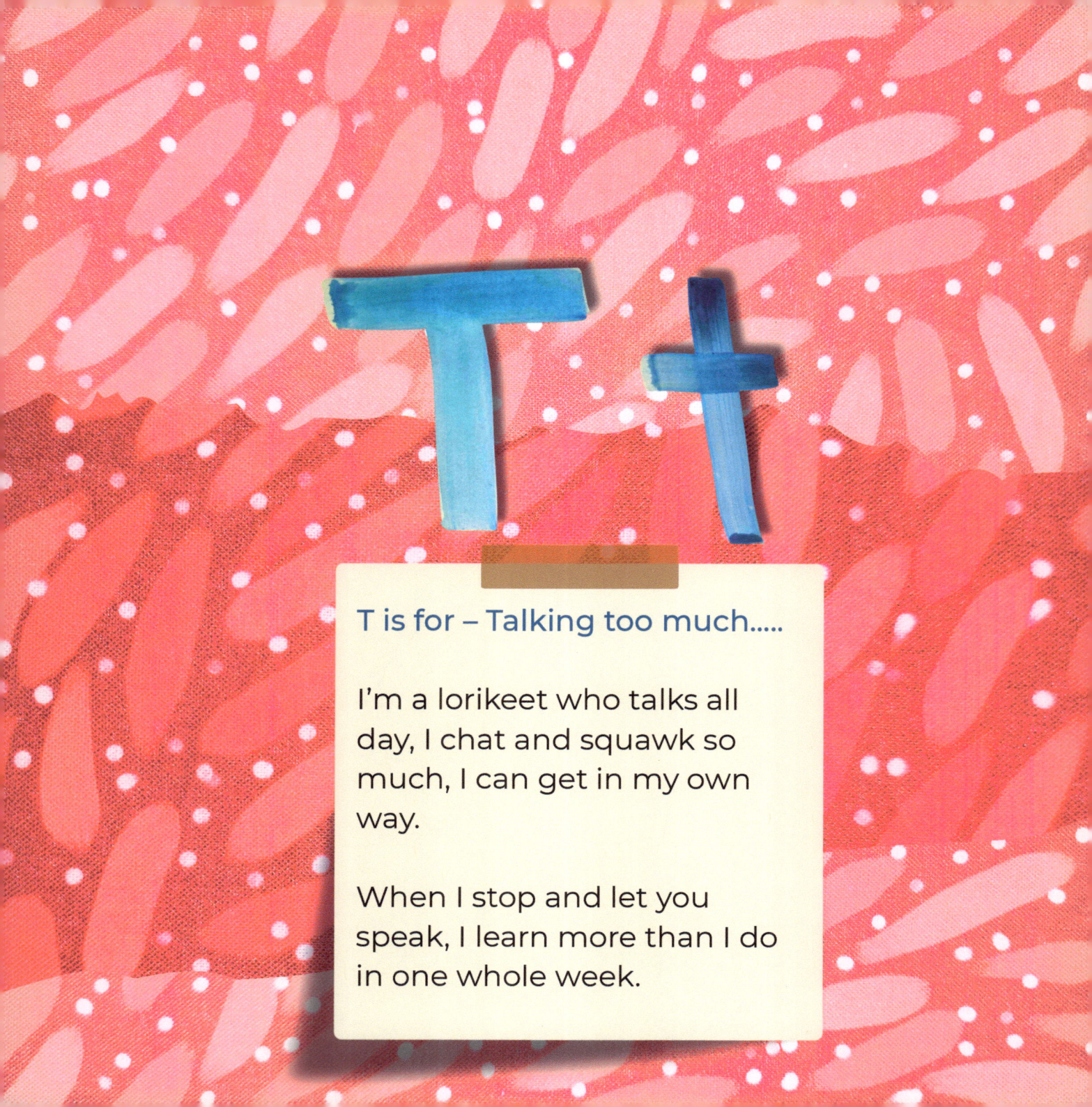

T is for – Talking too much…..

I'm a lorikeet who talks all day, I chat and squawk so much, I can get in my own way.

When I stop and let you speak, I learn more than I do in one whole week.

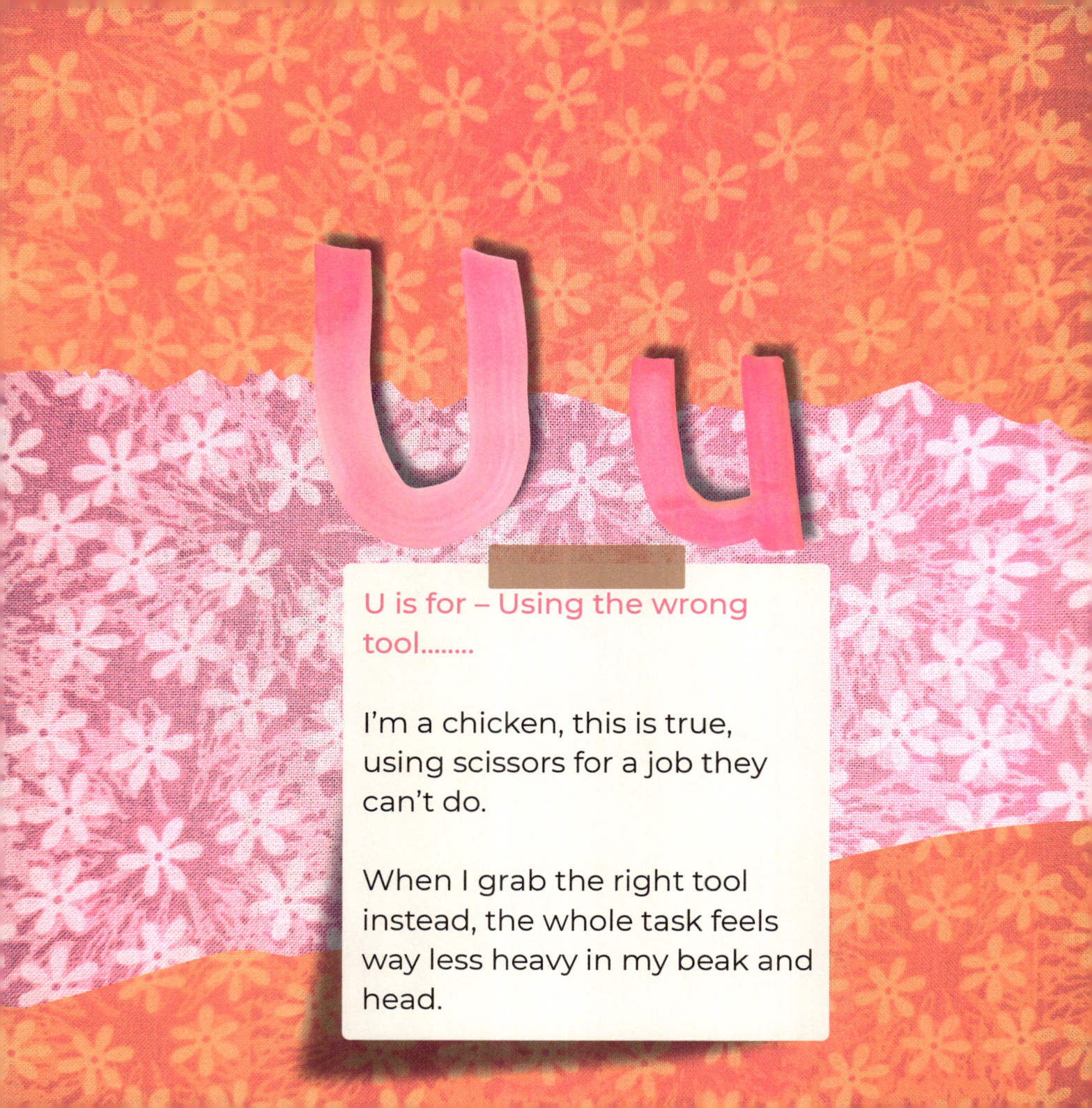

U is for – Using the wrong tool........

I'm a chicken, this is true, using scissors for a job they can't do.

When I grab the right tool instead, the whole task feels way less heavy in my beak and head.

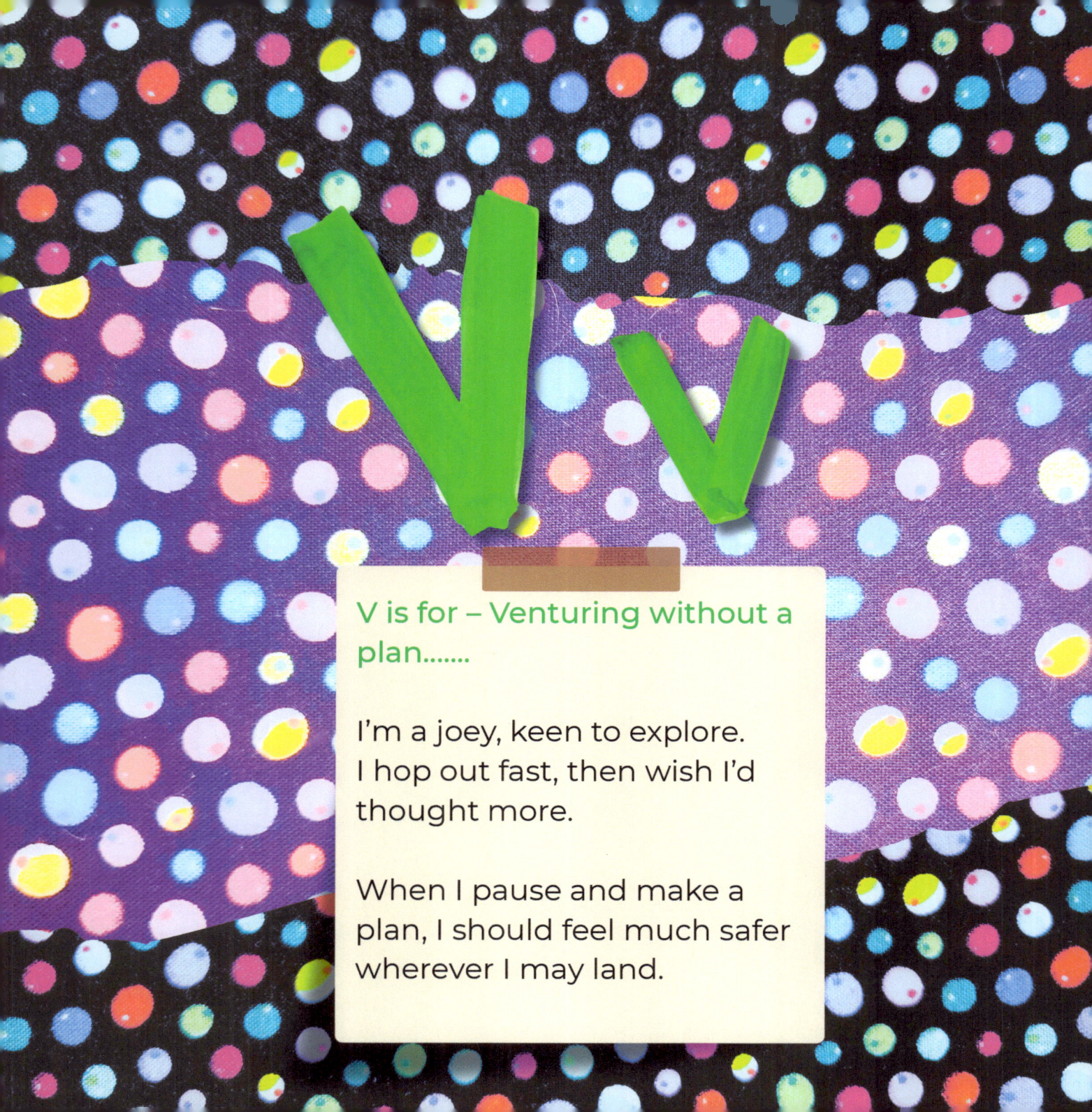

V is for – Venturing without a plan.......

I'm a joey, keen to explore.
I hop out fast, then wish I'd thought more.

When I pause and make a plan, I should feel much safer wherever I may land.

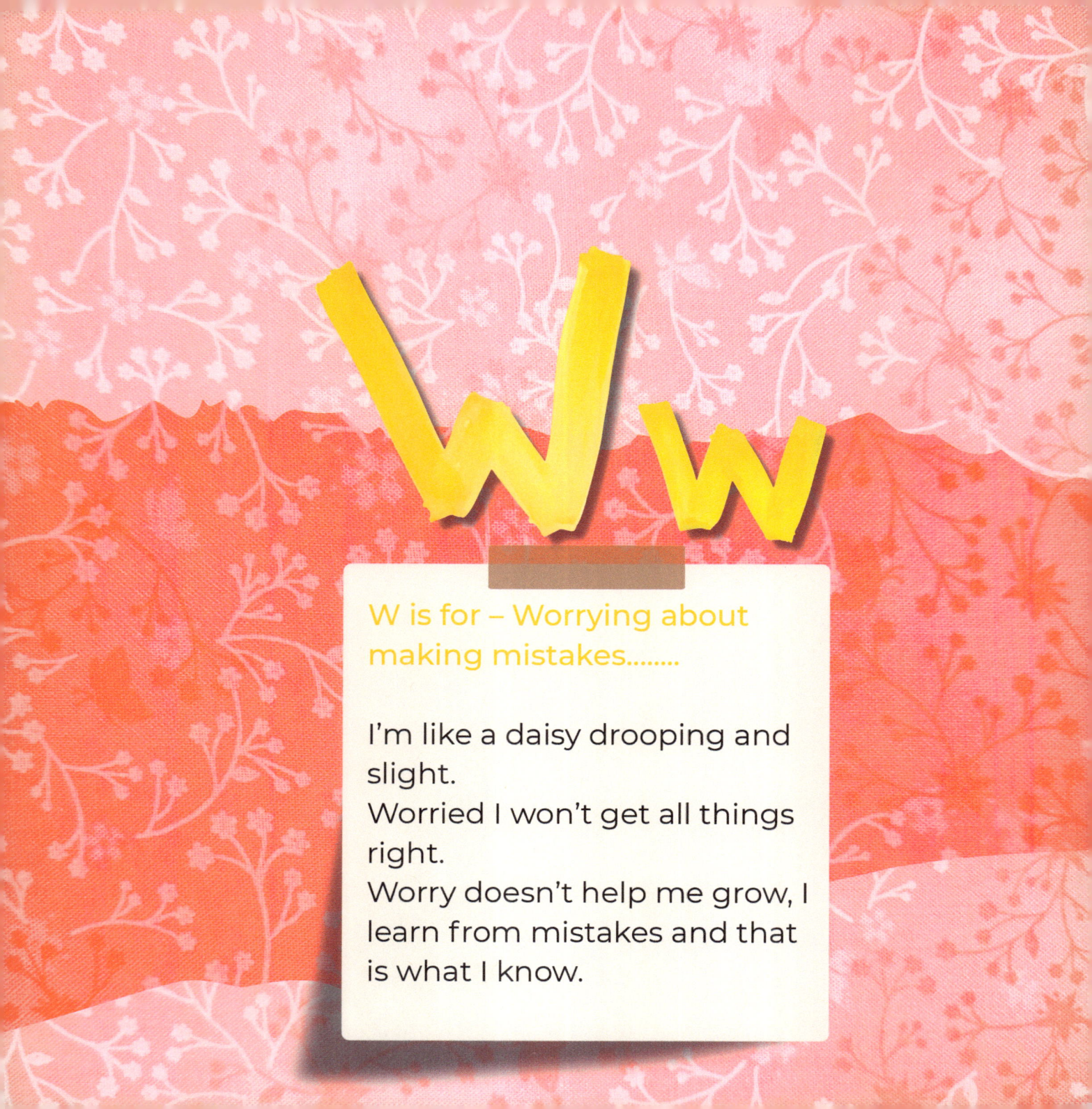

W is for – Worrying about making mistakes……..

I'm like a daisy drooping and slight.
Worried I won't get all things right.
Worry doesn't help me grow, I learn from mistakes and that is what I know.

X is for - eXpecting perfection.......

I see the flowers growing wild,
each flaw a quiet guide.
Even butterflies still fly with
wings a little torn at the side.
So, when I mess up,
I try to breathe and see,
perfection isn't real at all,
just progress in growing me.

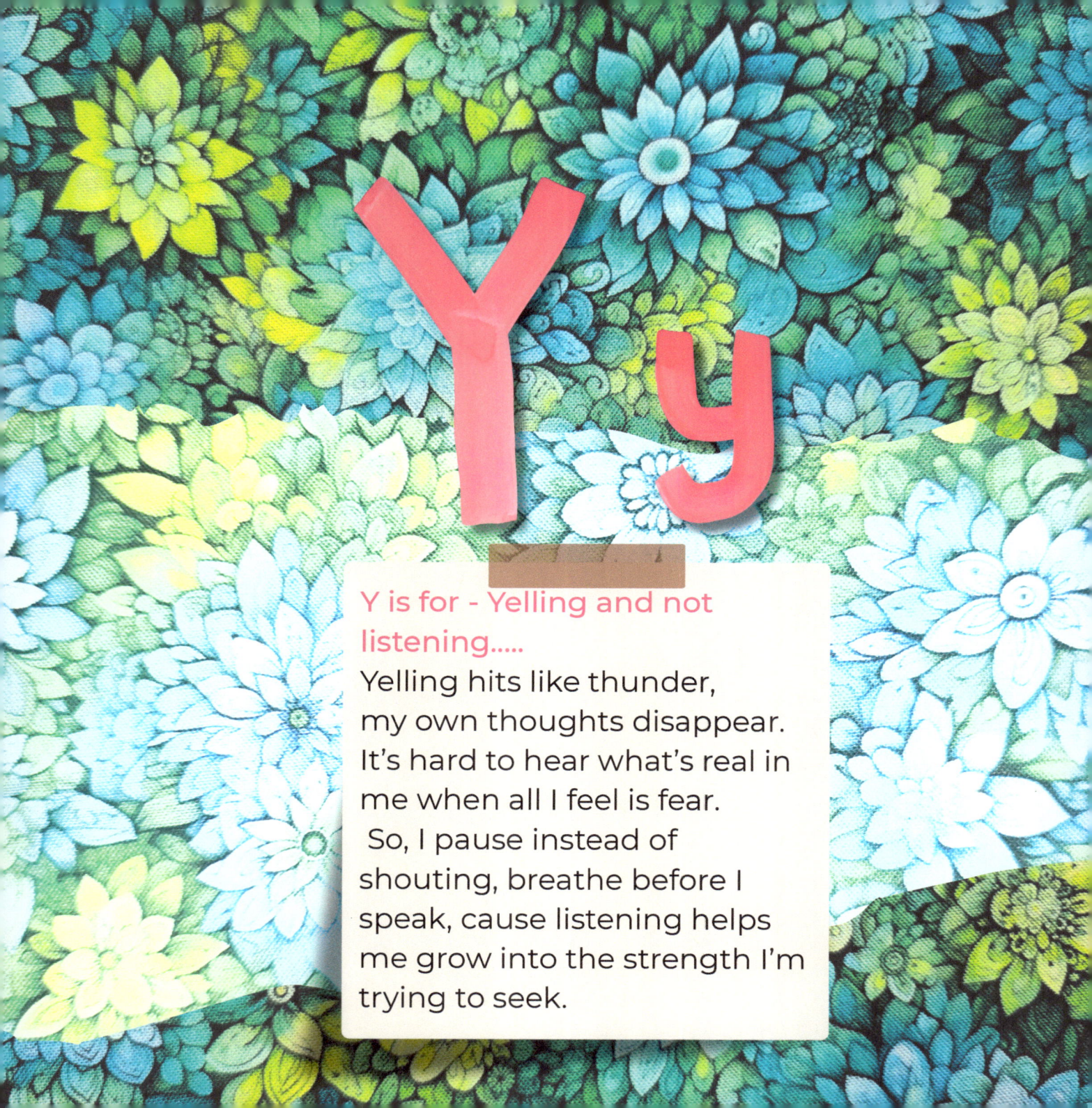

Y is for - Yelling and not listening.....

Yelling hits like thunder, my own thoughts disappear. It's hard to hear what's real in me when all I feel is fear. So, I pause instead of shouting, breathe before I speak, cause listening helps me grow into the strength I'm trying to seek.

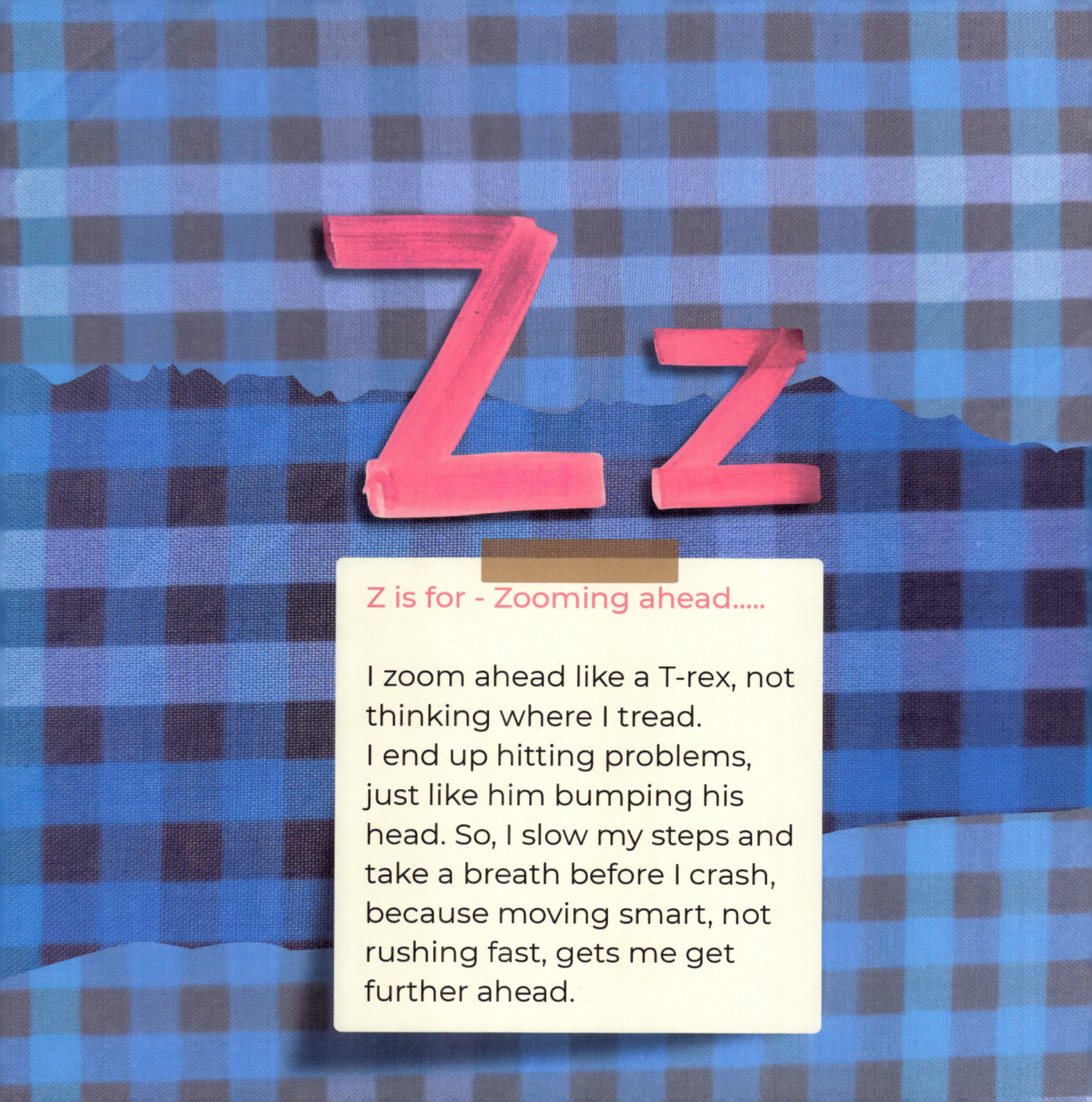

Z is for - Zooming ahead.....

I zoom ahead like a T-rex, not thinking where I tread.
I end up hitting problems, just like him bumping his head. So, I slow my steps and take a breath before I crash, because moving smart, not rushing fast, gets me get further ahead.

www.ingramcontent.com/pod-product-compliance
Lightning Source LLC
Chambersburg PA
CBHW041109070526
44583CB00003B/125